ABOUT ME

BY MARTI ABBOTT AND BETTY JANE POLK

FEARON TEACHER AIDS
Simon & Schuster Supplementary Education Group

Editor: Carol Williams
Copyeditor: Diane Sovljanski
Illustration: Tom McFarland
Design: Diann Abbott

ISBN 0-8224-0491-5

Printed in the United States of America
1. 9 8 7 6 5 4 3 2 1

Contents

How Do I Feel?

Introduction

All too often teachers read a book to children to entertain them or fill some spare moments, and that is the end of it. With the closing of the book, teachers shut out children's responses and ideas. Teachable moments are lost forever. The Books and Beyond series provides teachers with creative activities and critical-thinking stimulators to maximize the effectiveness of good literature. A piece of literature can become the basis for a learning unit that spans many areas of the curriculum.

Each lesson in the Books and Beyond series begins with a brief synopsis of the book and introductory ideas to stimulate student interest. After reading the book aloud, the use of the critical-thinking and discussion questions will help children draw from their own related experiences and analyze, evaluate, and apply the message of the book. Follow-up activities that center around many curriculum areas and include a variety of teaching styles will help children move beyond the book and internalize its message.

About Me is a collection of lessons based on children's books that deal specifically with children's experiences and their feelings about themselves and the world around them. Children will naturally relate to the characters and scenarios described in this collection of stories. As children begin to see their own value, potential, and unique qualities, they will develop a more positive self-image and the confidence they need to handle real-life situations.

Dandelion

Written and illustrated by Don Freeman
New York: Viking Press, 1964

Synopsis

Dandelion receives a party invitation and decides to change his outward appearance by getting a new hairdo and new clothes before attending the party. However, when he arrives at the party, his friends don't recognize him. He promises from then on to be "just plain me!"

Introduction

Make a party invitation and seal it in an envelope. Open the envelope in front of the children and let them know that you have been invited to a party. Ask the children for their suggestions about how you should prepare for the party. They might suggest that you buy a gift, decide on what you will wear, or plan how you will get there. Invite the children to listen closely as the story is read aloud to find out how Dandelion prepares for the party he has been invited to attend.

Critical-Thinking and Discussion Questions

1. Dandelion was very excited when he received the party invitation in the mail. His first concern was how he would look at the party. What is the first thing you think about when you receive an invitation?
2. Why do you think Dandelion was so concerned about his appearance? Do you think Dandelion looked better before or after he had his hair done and bought new clothes? Why?
3. Jennifer Giraffe didn't recognize Dandelion when he came knocking on her door, so she shut the door without letting him in. How would you have felt if you had been Dandelion?
4. Dandelion wanted to change the way he looked. Have you ever wanted to change the way you look? What would you change if you could? Why?
5. Dandelion realized that his friends liked him just the way he was. Do you like your friends just the way they are? Do you think your friends like you just the way you are? How do you know?

Creative Writing Starters
Language Arts

The last time I had my hair cut I _____.

New clothes make me look _____.

At a party it is fun to _____.

I like my friends just the way they are because _____ .

Story Titles

What a Surprise!

The Most Unusual Party

My New Look

You're Invited
Language Arts

Ask children to think about the important information that should be included on a party invitation, such as the time, date, and place of the party, the type of party, and who is giving the party. Make a list on the chalkboard. Many invitations include an R.S.V.P. (abbreviation for the French words *Respondez s'il vous plait*) and although Jennifer Giraffe doesn't include it, you might want to discuss its meaning and purpose. Give each child a copy of the party invitation reproducible on page 12. Invite children to fill in the information for their very own party, add designs to fit the theme of the party, and then fold each invitation so that it opens like a book.

Let's Pretend
Language Arts

For younger children, set up a dramatic play center equipped with beauty or barber shop supplies:

empty shampoo bottles	curlers
towels	blow-dryers
dishpan for basin	empty razors
clips, barrettes, and hairnets	nail files
brushes and combs	

Include dress-up clothes, hats, handbags, and shoes so that children can pretend they are preparing to go to a party just as Dandelion did.

Lion Mask
Art

Reproduce the "Lion Mask" on page 13 on yellow construction paper for each child. Children add details to the mask with crayons and then cut out the mask and the inner eyes. Use an X-acto knife to cut the dotted line around the nose for each child. Give each child a handful of 3" x ¹/₂" strips of yellow construction paper. Children glue the strips all around the outer edge of the mask to make the lion's mane. They can give their lion a hairdo much like Dandelion's by curling the strips around a pencil. Give the children each a large rubber band that they can cut to make one long, stretchy band. Staple the band to each side of the mask.

Dandelion's Day
Math

Give each child a copy of the "Dandelion's Day" reproducible on page 14. After students have completed the word problems, encourage them to write some original word problems about Dandelion's day on the back of their papers. When the papers are collected, read some of the original word problems aloud and call on volunteers to solve them.

Verne's Ferns & Flowers
Science

Dandelion bought a bouquet of dandelions from Verne's Ferns & Flowers shop. Display a real dandelion or a picture of one and point out some interesting facts about the flower:

   The name *dandelion* comes from a French word that means lion's tooth.
   Dandelion leaves can be used in salads, or they can be cooked.
   Dandelion blossoms open in the morning and close in the evening.
Encourage children to choose one of their favorite flowers and do a little research to discover some interesting facts to share with the class.

Date:_____

Time:_____

Place:_____

Given by:_____

party!

_____

You are invited to a

About Me © 1991 Fearon Teacher Aids

Lion Mask

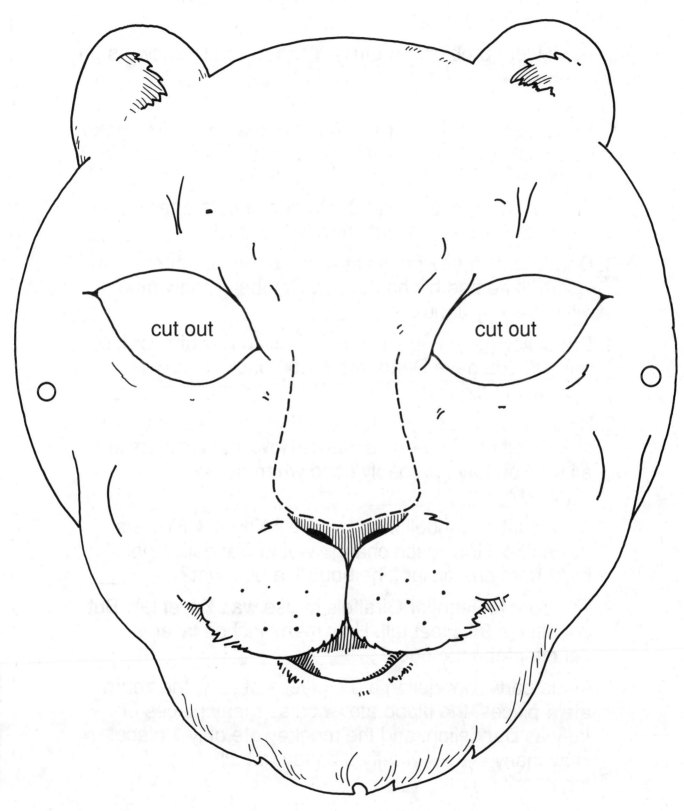

cut out

cut out

Dandelion

Dandelion's Day

Read each word problem carefully. Then write the answers on the blanks.

1. Dandelion went to bed at 8:00 on Friday night. He woke up at 6:00 on Saturday morning. How many hours did he sleep?_____

2. Dandelion exercised for 20 minutes. If he started exercising at 8:15 a.m., what time did he finish? _____

3. Dandelion's mane grows at a rate of $1/2$ inch per month. If he had his hair cut on October 1, how much will it grow by January 1? _____

4. Dandelion gave Lou a five-dollar bill to pay him for his haircut. Lou gave Dandelion $1.50 back in change. How much did Dandelion's haircut cost? _____

5. By the time Lou had used 12 curlers, he had only rolled half of Dandelion's mane. How many curlers in all will Lou have probably used when he is finished?_____

6. A bouquet of dandelions at Verne's Ferns & Flowers costs 75¢. How much change would Dandelion get back from one dollar if he bought a bouquet?_____

7. The door to Jennifer Giraffe's house was 7 feet tall. But Jennifer is 9 $1/2$ feet tall. How many inches taller is Jennifer than the door?_____

8. At the party, Dandelion ate 4 pieces of taffy, the zebra ate 6 pieces, the hippo ate twice as many pieces of taffy as Dandelion, and the monkey ate only 1 piece. How many pieces of taffy did they eat all together?_____

About Me © 1991 Fearon Teacher Aids

Dandelion

Crow Boy

Written by Taro Yashima
New York: Viking Press, 1955

Synopsis

Chibi is always alone and silently observing others. At the end of elementary school, his classmates discover Chibi's special talent and begin to accept and understand his differences. The Japanese setting of the story exposes children to a culture different from their own.

Introduction

Show children the cover of *Crow Boy*. Ask them where they think the story takes place. The boy in the picture has a special talent, but a long time passes before his classmates discover what it is. Encourage children to listen as the story is read aloud to find out what his special talent is.

Critical-Thinking and Discussion Questions

1. The children in the village school gave Crow Boy the name Chibi. Why did the children give him that nickname? Has anyone ever given you a nickname? What was it? Why did they give you that name?
2. Chibi was left alone during study time and playtime. He felt like a tagalong. Have you ever felt all alone at school? What did you do? What do you do when you notice other children who are alone?
3. If you had been one of the children in the village school, how would you have treated Chibi?
4. What unique talent did Mr. Isobe discover Chibi had? Do you have a talent that you think not many people have? What is it?
5. The children did not like Crow Boy because he was different and they did not understand him. How do you feel when you meet someone who is very different from you? What are some ways that you could better understand someone who is **not** just like you?

Creative Writing Starters
Language Arts

When a new student comes into my class I _____ .
I feel all alone when _____ .
I think I am good at _____ .
My friend is different from me because he/she _____ .

Story Titles
My Hidden Talent
The First Day at My New School
Alone Again

I Am Special
Language Arts

Ask children to recall some of the things that Crow Boy could do really well. Encourage children to think of some special talents that they have or hobbies that they especially enjoy. Give each child a copy of the "Crow Boy and Me" reproducible on page 17. The children draw a picture of Crow Boy displaying a special ability and then make a list of their own creative or artistic talents. Encourage volunteers to demonstrate their talent for the class on a future date.

Patterned Rubbings
Science

Careful observation is essential to scientific study. Chibi observed his environment and discovered patterns and designs just as a scientist notices the intricate details of an object under study. Show children the book *Look Again!* by Tana Hoban. Then give each child a 4" x 5" sheet of thin white paper. Have children make rubbings of a textured object in the classroom (paper clip, coin, leaf, rubber band, wall, tile floor) by placing the paper over the object and rubbing the paper with the side of a crayon. Collect the rubbings. Divide the class into groups of four and give each group four rubbings. Encourage the group to work together to discover what objects were used to make the rubbings.

Black and White
Art

Show children Chibi's black-and-white drawing that Mr. Isobe tacked up on the wall for other students to admire. Give each child a sheet of white drawing paper and a black crayon, a piece of charcoal, or black paint and a paintbrush. Encourage students to design unique pictures. Give each student a copy of the "Japanese" reproducible on page 18 to practice writing some Japanese characters on their pictures. Explain to children that Japanese is usually written from top to bottom and from right to left.

Crow Boy and Me

Draw a picture of Crow Boy doing something he was good at.

Make a list of your talents or hobbies.

_____

_____

_____

_____

_____

_____

_____

_____

Japanese

Japanese is usually written from top to bottom and from left to right. When done properly, it is written with a paintbrush and black ink on rice paper. Try writing the Japanese numbers from one to ten and the Japanese characters for the word *Japan*.

ichi	roku
一	六
one	six
ni	**shichi**
二	七
two	seven
san	**hachi**
三	八
three	eight
shi	**ku**
四	九
four	nine
go	**juu**
五	十
five	ten

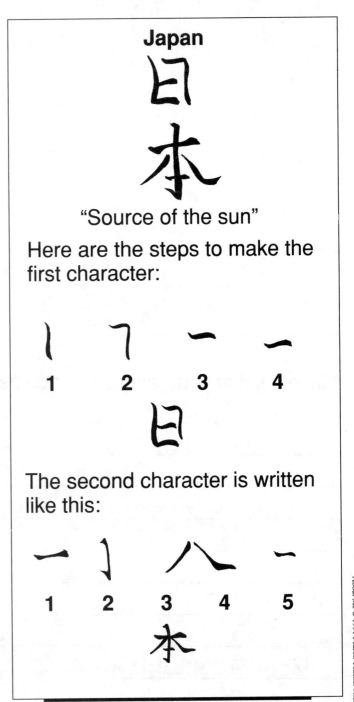

Japan

日
本

"Source of the sun"

Here are the steps to make the first character:

The second character is written like this:

About Me © 1991 Fearon Teacher Aids

Crow Boy

The Story of Ferdinand

Written by Munro Leaf and illustrated by Robert Lawson
New York: Viking Press, 1936

Synopsis

Ferdinand is a friendly bull who loves to sit under his favorite tree and smell flowers. But one day he finds himself the center of attention at a bullfight. The audience expects Ferdinand to be a fierce fighter, but Ferdinand finds the flowers in the ladies' hair more interesting than the matador and his red cape.

Introduction

Point out Spain and its capital, Madrid, on a world map. Give children a brief explanation of the bullfighting custom. Explain that Ferdinand is not like most other bulls. Ask children to listen as the story is read aloud to find out how Ferdinand is different.

Critical-Thinking and Discussion Questions

1. The five men realized at the bullfight that Ferdinand was not the kind of bull they had first thought he was. Have you ever found out that someone was really quite different from the way you first imagined them to be after you got to know them? What was your first impression of them and why did it change? Do people often get the wrong first impression of you? Why?

2. Ferdinand was not like other bulls. Do you ever think you are not like other children your age? If so, how are you different? Do you think it is OK to be different, or should you try to be like everyone else? What did Ferdinand think about being different?

3. Imagine you are Ferdinand sitting in the middle of that huge arena and you know that everyone has come to see a bullfight. Would you just sit there and smell the flowers as Ferdinand did or would you fight the men? Why?

4. What is one word you would use to describe Ferdinand? What is one word you would use to describe yourself? How are you different from Ferdinand and how are you like him?

5. The men had to take Ferdinand home because he would not fight. What do you think happened in the arena after Ferdinand left?

Creative Writing Starters

Language Arts

When I want to do something different from the rest of my friends,
I _____ .
If I sat on a bee, I would _____ .
When people first meet me they think _____ .
I would rather smell flowers than _____ .

Story Titles
I'm Not Usually Like This!
The Brave Bullfighter
My Most Unusual Hat

The Story of Ferdinand

Language Arts

Give each child a copy of "The Story of Ferdinand" reproducible on page 22 and two sheets of white drawing paper. Have children stack the two sheets of drawing paper on top of each other and fold them once lengthwise and once the other way to make an 8-page booklet. Have children trim the long, folded edge to separate the pages and put two staples on the short, folded end. Children can write "The Story of Ferdinand" on the front page. Have children cut the sentences apart and glue one on each page of their booklet to retell the story of Ferdinand in the correct sequence:

> Once upon a time there was a bull named Ferdinand who liked to
> smell flowers.
> One day five men came to pick the roughest bull.
> Ferdinand sat on a bumblebee.
> The men chose Ferdinand and took him to Madrid in a cart.
> Ferdinand just sat in the bullfighting ring and smelled the flowers.
> The Matador was so mad he cried.
> They had to take Ferdinand back to his home.

Children can add illustrations to their booklets.

What Do You Think?
Language Arts

Have children choose partners and give each pair a copy of the "What Do You Think?" reproducible on page 23. Encourage partners to work together to recall parts of the story that fit each category. Share answers orally when all the children have finished.

Fancy Hats
Art

Show the children the page in *The Story of Ferdinand* with the five men in their funny hats. Help children notice some of the unique features about each hat. Give each child a hat pattern reproducible on page 24 and a 12" x 18" sheet of colored construction paper. Children choose one of the two hat patterns or make up their own original pattern to trace and cut out on the folded sheet of construction paper. Have children cut the slit and reinforce the ends of the slit with tape after unfolding the hat. Encourage children to decorate their hats in a unique way.

Flower Fun
Science and Math

Ask each child to bring a flower to school. Identify and write the name of each flower on a class graph. The students can enjoy smelling the flowers as Ferdinand did, and then you can record on the graph how many children liked the smell of each flower.

The Story of Ferdinand

Cut the sentences apart and glue them in the correct order in your booklet.

Ferdinand sat on a bumblebee.

- -

They had to take Ferdinand back to his home.

- -

Ferdinand just sat in the bullfighting ring and smelled the flowers.

- -

The Matador was so mad he cried.

- -

Once upon a time there was a bull named Ferdinand who liked to smell flowers.

- -

One day five men came to pick the roughest bull.

- -

The men chose Ferdinand and took him to Madrid in a cart.

About Me © 1991 Fearon Teacher Aids

Name _____

What Do You Think?

Try to remember a part from *The Story of Ferdinand* that you think fits each category below. Write it on the lines.

MOST BELIEVABLE

MOST UNBELIEVABLE

MOST HUMOROUS

MOST EXCITING

MOST FRIGHTENING

About Me © 1991 Fearon Teacher Aids

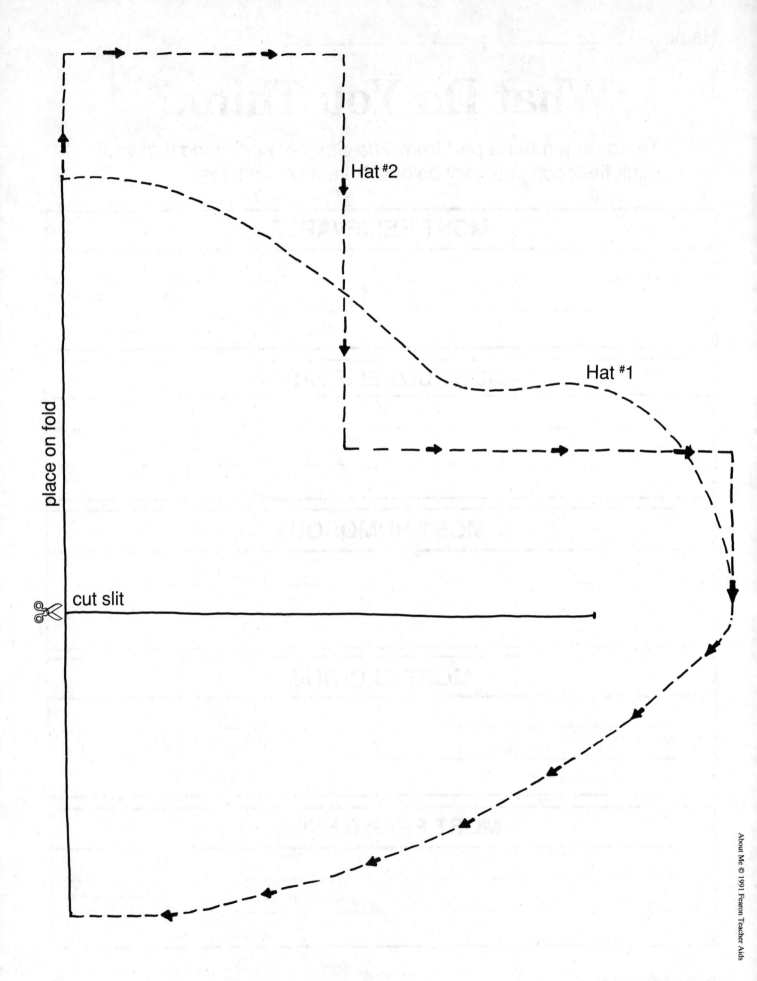

place on fold

cut slit

Hat #2

Hat #1

The Story of Ferdinand

About Me © 1991 Fearon Teacher Aids

Pocketful of Cricket

Written by Rebecca Caudill and illustrated by Evaline Ness
New York: Holt, Rinehart and Winston, 1964

Synopsis

Jay is a young farm boy who enjoys all the sights and sounds around him. One day, near the end of summer, Jay takes a cricket home to keep as a pet. When school starts, Jay decides to take the cricket with him in his pocket on the first day. Jay's teacher is very understanding of Jay's fondness for his new pet and encourages him to share it with the whole class.

Introduction

Invite children to pretend that they have a small animal or insect in their pockets. Ask individual children to imitate the sound it would make and have the rest of the class guess what is in the child's pocket. Ask the children what sound they would hear if a cricket were in your pocket. The boy in the story has a pocketful of cricket. Encourage children to listen carefully as the story is read aloud to find out what sound Jay's pet cricket makes and what happens to his pet.

Critical-Thinking and Discussion Questions

1. One day Jay took longer than usual to get to the pasture because he was having so much fun seeing, feeling, smelling, and hearing everything around him. Can you remember some of the things that interested Jay on his walk? What were they? Which of those things would be most interesting to you? Why?
2. Jay decided to keep a cricket he found as a pet. He gave it a cage, some special food to eat, and some water. Have you ever tried to keep an animal or insect you found as a pet? What did the pet need that you had to provide? How long were you able to keep it? What happened?
3. Why do you think Jay decided to take his cricket to school? Would you have taken it to school? Why or why not?
4. Jay hoped that nobody would notice the cricket in his pocket. Have you ever put something in your pocket that you hoped nobody would notice? Were you able to keep it a secret? Can you tell us your secret now? What was it?
5. What was the teacher's reaction to the cricket? Do you think she handled the situation well? Why or why not?
6. How would the situation have been different if the teacher had forced Jay to let his cricket go? What do you think might have happened?

Creative Writing Starters

Language Arts

I would like to have a pet _____.
The best thing about a pocket is _____ .
One day when I went for a walk I found _____ .
If I had a cricket, I would feed it _____ .

Story Titles
Secret in My Pocket
Trouble on the Bus
Sshh, Listen!

Show-and-Tell

Language Arts

Jay shared his cricket with the class at "Show-and-Tell" time. If you don't already have a regularly scheduled "Show-and-Tell" time, this would be a good opportunity to begin one. It is a valuable experience for children to speak in front of their classmates. Children enjoy sharing special items that are of interest to them, and "Show-and-Tell" enables classmates to get to know each other a bit better. If you already have a scheduled time, give students some specific instructions for the next time they participate.

- Share with the class something small enough to fit under a glass.
- Capture an insect or draw a picture of one and put it in a cage or under a glass. Research the insect to find out a few interesting facts to share with the class.
- Jay decided that he would bring beans for "Show-and-Tell" next time. Think of an interesting way to share beans. You might want to make a collage using beans, tell about the different types of beans, or share a favorite recipe that uses beans.

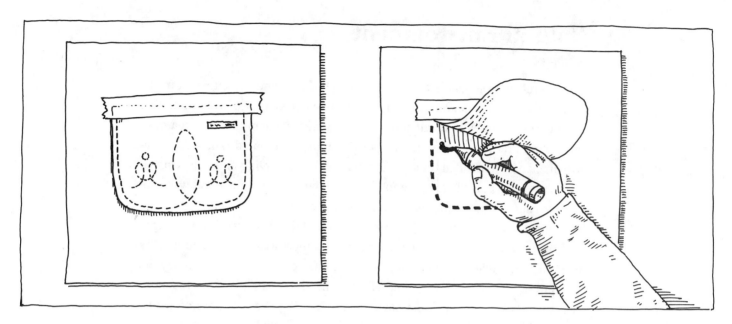

A Pocketful Of ?

Language Arts

Encourage students to imagine what they would like to take to school in their pockets. Have each student think of one idea and keep it in mind. Give each student a copy of the "A Pocketful Of ?" reproducible on page 29 and a 5" square piece of colored construction paper. Have students round two adjacent corners of the construction paper to make a pocket shape and place it on the bottom section of the reproducible. Place a 5" strip of tape over the top of the pocket to create a flap that can be lifted. The children decorate the outside of the pocket and then draw a secret picture underneath the flap and write the name of what they would like to put in their pockets. Invite students to write on the lines at the top of the paper five sentences that describe what is in their pocket. When everyone is finished, each child can read his or her description, and classmates can guess what is in the pocket. Or, display the colorful pocket pages on a bulletin board and encourage students to read the clues, make guesses, and lift the pocket flaps on their own.

Cricket Cards

Science

Have students choose partners for a scientific tic-tac-toe game. Give each pair of students a copy of the "Cricket Cards" reproducible on page 30 and a blank sheet of paper. (Reproduce the "Cricket Cards" on construction paper to prevent students from reading the words on the backs of the cards.) Have students cut the cards apart and draw a tic-tac-toe grid on the blank paper. One player reads a cricket card to his or her partner. The partner must tell whether the statement is true or false. If the partner is correct, he or she can place an X on the tic-tac-toe board. If the partner is incorrect, the player who read the card can place an O on the tic-tac-toe. The players take turns reading cards to each other until one player has three X's or O's in a row.

Natural Environment

Science

Our natural environment is made up of everything around us that is not man-made. Jay closely observed his natural environment as he was walking to the pasture. Ask children to recall some of the natural wonders Jay saw, heard, smelled, and felt, and write their responses on the chalkboard. The natural environment can be divided into two general categories: living and nonliving. Choose several students to come to the chalkboard one at a time and write an *L* for "living" or an *NL* for "nonliving" next to each item listed. Accompany the students on a walk to a nearby park or around the schoolyard. Encourage students to carefully observe the natural environment as Jay did when he took his walk. The students can also try out some different ways to walk as Jay did (forward or backward). When you return to the classroom, give the students each a sheet of white paper and have them title it "My Natural Environment." They can then fold the paper in half, open it up, and label one side "Living" and the other side "Nonliving." After the walk, encourage students to draw pictures of or write about their observations of the natural environment.

Name _____

A Pocketful Of ?

Use a 5" square piece of construction paper to make a pocket at the bottom of the paper. Put a piece of tape across the top of the pocket to make a flap that can be lifted. Decide what you would like to take to school in your pocket and draw a picture of it underneath the pocket flap. Write five sentences describing what is in your pocket.

_____

_____

_____

_____

_____

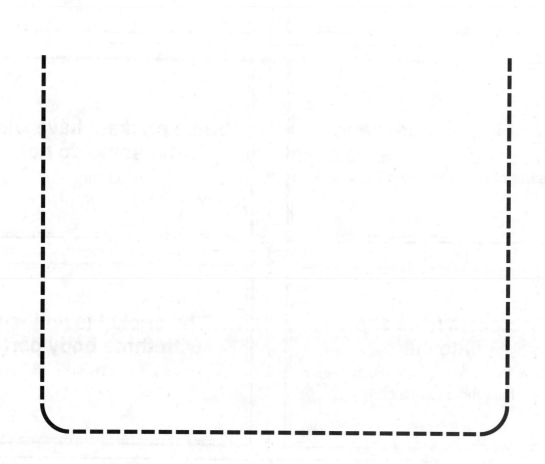

Cricket Cards

Only male crickets make sound.
(True)

Crickets hunt for food during the day.
(False, crickets hunt for food at night.)

Crickets look much like grasshoppers.
(True)

Crickets eat wool sweaters.
(True)

Crickets cannot hear.
(False, crickets have hearing organs in their front legs just below the knee.)

Some crickets have wings and some do not.
(True)

Crickets have short antennae.
(False, the antennae are much longer than the cricket's body.)

The cricket is an insect with three body parts.
(True)

About Me © 1991 Fearon Teacher Aids

Leo the Late Bloomer

Written by Robert Kraus and illustrated by Jose Aruego
New York: Windmill Books, 1971

Synopsis

Leo couldn't do anything right. At least, that is what he thought. Leo's mother patiently waited, and Leo's father watched for signs of change. In the end, Leo bloomed "in his own good time."

Introduction

Show children a picture of a rose and a tulip. Ask the children which one they like the best. The tulip blooms in the spring and the rose doesn't bloom until summer. Ask the children if they think the tulip is better because it blooms first. Flowers grow at different rates and so do people and animals. Encourage the children to listen carefully as the story is read aloud to find out how Leo grows and how he feels about it.

Critical-Thinking and Discussion Questions

1. Can you remember what Leo thought he couldn't do right? Are there some times when you feel as Leo did?
2. Leo's mother was not worried that Leo couldn't do things that others could do. She said that Leo was just a "late bloomer." Do you worry when you cannot do something that your friends can do? What does it mean to be a "late bloomer"?
3. Leo's father kept watching him, hoping to see some changes. Leo's mother told Leo's father that "A watched bloomer doesn't bloom." What do you think that means? (Discuss with children the saying, "A watched pot never boils," or discuss how slowly time passes when you watch the clock.)
4. One day, "in his own good time," Leo bloomed. You learn and grow "in your own good time," too. What are some abilities you might have next year that you do not have now? What abilities do you have now that you did not have last year?
5. Compare yourself to Leo. In what ways are you like him? In what ways are you different?

Creative Writing Starters

Language Arts

When my friends are doing something I cannot do, I feel _____ .

If I were Leo, I would _____ .

I hope that I will be able to _____ soon.

I feel the same way Leo did when I try to _____ .

Story Titles

I Made It!

Better Late Than Never

How to Be Patient

Letters to Leo

Language Arts

Give each child a copy of the letter form reproducible on page 34. Have children write letters of encouragement to Leo. Children can include personal experiences they have had being "late bloomers," hints on being patient, and anything else that might help cheer Leo.

Three-Line Writing

Art

Show children the picture of Leo writing and ask them to think of a way that they could write three lines at one time the way Leo did. Suggest that children tape three different-colored crayons or markers together, making sure the points are even. Encourage children to create interesting and unique designs.

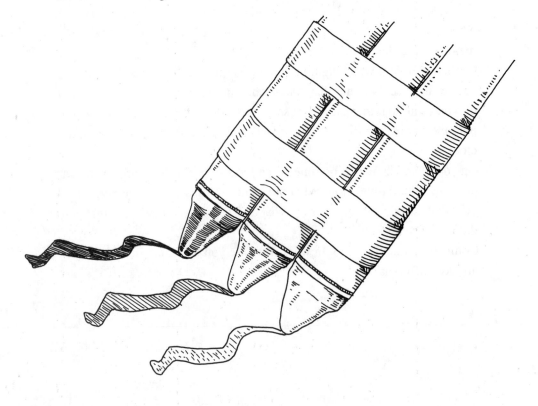

Add-On Art

Art

Show children the picture Leo and his friends drew together. Give the children each a sheet of drawing paper and have them begin drawing a picture. After two minutes, the children exchange papers and add to the new picture they now have. Let another two minutes go by before the children exchange papers again. Repeat the process four or five times to complete each picture.

How Long?

Math

Leo bloomed "in his own good time." Give children practice estimating the length of time necessary to complete tasks. Give each child four 3" x 5" cards. Have children write *years*, *days*, *minutes*, or *hours* on each card. Ask the children how long it would take to do various tasks. Have each of them hold up a 3" x 5" card with the appropriate word to show their answers.
Ask children to estimate how long it would take to:

> brush their teeth
> grow 5 inches taller
> watch three television shows
> sprout a seed
> eat dinner
> write a sentence
> write their name
> get a good night's sleep
> learn to read

_____

Date

Dear Leo,

_____

_____

_____

_____

_____

_____

_____

_____

_____

_____

_____

_____

Your friend,

_____

About Me © 1991 Fearon Teacher Aids

Just Me

Written and illustrated by Marie Hall Ets
New York: Viking Press, 1965

Synopsis

A little boy tries to imitate the motions and actions of many animals. He tries walking like a cat, hopping like a rabbit, wriggling like a snake, and leaping like a frog. But, he eventually ends up running like nobody else—"JUST ME"—to catch up to his dad who is pulling away from shore in a boat.

Introduction

Ask children if they have ever tried to copy what someone else was doing. Invite children to copy some simple movement patterns. Clap your hands twice, tap your feet twice, and then clap again. The little boy in the story tries to copy what some of the animals are doing. Encourage children to listen carefully as the story is read aloud to find out which animals the boy copies.

Critical-Thinking and Discussion Questions

1. What are some of the animals that the little boy tried to copy? Which of those animals would you most like to copy? Why?
2. Which of the animals was the boy unable to copy? Why? Which of the animals mentioned do you think was the hardest to copy? Why?
3. Do you think this story is real or make-believe? Why?
4. The little boy realized that the way he walked and ran was just right for him. Do you think the way you do things is just right for you, or would you rather be like someone else? Have you ever tried to be like someone else by copying the way they walk, talk, or dress?
5. The little boy ran "like nobody else" to catch his dad before the boat pulled away. Where do you think the boy and his dad went in the boat?

Creative Writing Starters
Language Arts

My favorite animal is _____ because _____.
I can run faster than _____.
I am glad that I am "just me" because _____.
A pig would/would not make a good pet because _____ .

Story Titles
Hop, Climb, Wriggle
Copycat
If I Could Fly

What Am I?
Language Arts

Write the names of the twelve animals mentioned in the book on separate slips of paper. Put all the slips in a paper sack. Choose one student to come to the front of the classroom and draw a slip of paper from the sack. Have that student pantomime the actions of the animal while other students try to guess what it is. The student who guesses correctly can be the next silent actor or actress.

What If
Language Arts

In the story, the little boy imitates several animals. Ask the children to imagine what it would be like if animals tried to imitate people. Read *Animals Should Definitely Not Act Like People* and *Animals Should Definitely Not Wear Clothing* by Judi Barrett. These books present a humorous view of the problems animals would face if they were expected to behave and dress as people do.

Animimingo
Science

Reinforce students' knowledge of scientific facts about farm animals by playing this animal bingo game. Give each child a copy of the bingo card reproducible on page 38 and some game markers, such as buttons, beans, or macaroni. Write the names of the twelve animals from the book on the chalkboard. Have children copy one name in each box on their bingo cards in a random order.

cat	snake	turtle
rooster	cow	squirrel
pig	goose	goat
rabbit	horse	frog

Give clues about the animals by using facts from the book, such as "This animal likes to take a bath-and-nap in the mud." Each child checks his or her card for the matching animal name and covers the appropriate bingo square with a marker. Continue to play until one child shouts "Animingo" after covering all the squares in a horizontal or vertical row. Substitute clues from the book with other facts about these animals, such as animal colors, movements, products, and terms for their young.

How Big?
Math

Write a list of the twelve animals from the story on the chalkboard. Discuss the size and weight of each by asking the children questions about the animals:

Which animals do you think you could pick up and carry?

Which animals would fit inside a car?

Which animals do you think weigh less than you? Which animals weigh more?

As a class, have students order the list of animals on the chalkboard from the lightest to the heaviest.

CAT   SNAKE   TURTLE

ROOSTER   COW   SQUIRREL

PIG   GOOSE   GOAT

RABBIT   HORSE   FROG

Name _____

Animimgo

About Me © 1991 Fearon Teacher Aids

No Good in Art

Written by Miriam Cohen and illustrated by Lillian Hoban
New York: Greenwillow Books, 1980

Synopsis

Jim thought he was not good in art because the teacher showed him the right way to do everything. Another year and another teacher convinced him that he wasn't so bad after all.

Introduction

Ask children if they like to draw or paint pictures. Ask them what they like to draw the best, or if they sometimes feel like they just can't draw very well. Show children the picture on the cover of the book. Ask them what they think the little blond-haired boy is thinking. Encourage children to listen carefully as the story is read aloud to see how that little boy feels about painting and why.

Critical-Thinking and Discussion Questions

1. The first-grade art teacher asked the children to paint pictures of what they wanted to be when they got big. What did Jim's classmates want to be? What would you like to be when you get big?
2. Jim didn't want to paint a picture because he thought he was no good in art. Do you ever feel that you are no good at something? What do you think you are not good at? Why do you feel that way? How do you think you could become better at it?
3. All of the children admired Jim's picture when the teacher put it on display. How do you think Jim felt when his friends told him they thought he could be an artist? Can you remember a time when a friend said some nice things to you that made you feel really good? When was that and what did he or she say?
4. At the end of the story, Jim believed that he could be an artist. He felt very proud of his picture. What have you made that you felt very proud of?
5. How do you think Jim will feel the next time the art teacher tells the children to paint a picture? What kind of picture do you think Jim might paint?

Creative Writing Starters

Language Arts

When I paint a picture, I _____ .

If someone tells me my picture is ugly, I _____ .

I think I am really good at _____ .

I wish I were better at _____ .

My favorite thing to draw is _____ .

Story Titles

Disaster in Art Class

When I Grow Up

(Your Name), the Artist

Flower Faces

Art

Give the children another chance to look at the flower faces on the inside covers of the book. Then give them each a copy of the "Flower Faces" reproducible on page 42. Children can make flower faces the way Louie did in the story by painting or coloring the flower centers and petals and then adding facial features. Encourage originality and creativity.

What Will I Be?

Art

Invite children to paint pictures of what they want to be when they "get big." Give support and praise, and avoid correcting their work! Display the finished pictures and encourage children to make positive comments to one another about the paintings.

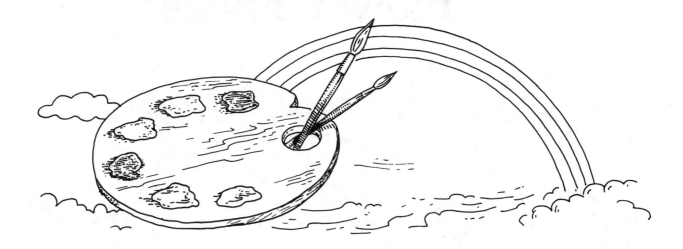

Wheel of Color

Art

Ask children to recall the colors Jim mixed to create green when he was
painting his picture. Give each child a copy of the "Color Wheel" reproducible on page 43. Have the children paint the labeled sections with blue, red,
and yellow paint. Then children can mix the two colors that are on each side
of a blank section and paint the blank section with the color they have made
(green, purple, or orange). Children can mix colors on pieces of waxed paper,
using cotton swabs rather than paintbrushes. Be sure children use a new
cotton swab each time they dip into a new color of paint.

Job Jargon

Social Studies

Ask children to recall some of the occupations mentioned by Jim's friends in
art class. Give each child a copy of the "People in Our Community" reproducible on page 44. Have children cut the pictures apart and glue one next to
each occupation title. The students draw a line from each occupation title
on the left of the page to the job description on the right.

Who Am I?

Social Studies

As children recall the names of the occupations mentioned in the book, list
them on the chalkboard. Ask children to contribute names of other occupations and add them to the list also. Choose one child to come to the front of
the room and pantomime one of the occupations. Invite the other children to
guess which one it is. The child who guesses correctly can be the next actor or
actress.

Flower Faces

No Good in Art

Color Wheel

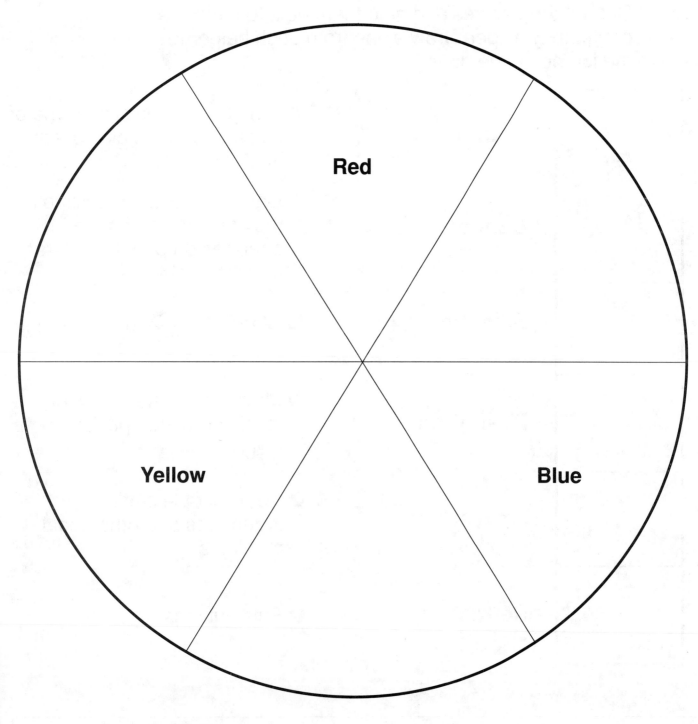

Red

Yellow

Blue

People in Our Community

Cut out the pictures and glue them next to the correct community helper. Draw a line from each helper to the job he or she does.

Doctor

Dancer

Scientist

Firefighter

Lawyer

Dentist

- A marine biologist is a type of scientist who studies ocean life.

- Can give people medicine if they are sick and often operates on people to cure medical problems.

- Cleans teeth and fills cavities.

- Moves his or her body to music and often performs on stage.

- Helps people settle arguments and other legal problems.

- Puts out fires.

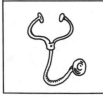   

About Me © 1991 Fearon Teacher Aids

No Good in Art

The Do-Something Day

Written by Joe Lasker
New York: Viking Press, 1982

Synopsis

Bernie wants to be helpful. But after a few "not nows," Bernie feels un-wanted and decides to run away. As he stops to say good-bye to his friends, they each ask Bernie to help out. Bernie ends up helping his family in ways he didn't even realize.

Introduction

Ask the children what they do when they wake up on a Saturday morning and the sun is shining brightly. The author of this book calls days like that "do-something" days. Encourage children to listen closely as the story is read aloud to find out what Bernie does on his "do-something" day.

Critical-Thinking and Discussion Questions

1. Bernie got mad because he felt that no one needed him. He wanted to run away. Have you ever had the feeling that no one needed you? What made you feel that way? What did you do?
2. Bernie ended up helping many people while he was running away. Who were some of the people Bernie helped and what jobs did he do for them? If you were Bernie, which of those jobs would you have enjoyed doing the most? Why?
3. Bernie helped his family because they found many uses for the things he had collected on his trip. How do you think Bernie felt at the end of the story? How do you feel after you have helped someone?
4. Mutt became Bernie's new pet. How do you think Bernie's life will be different now that he has a puppy?
5. What do you think Bernie will do the next time his parents or brother say "not now" to him? What do you do when someone tells you they don't have time for you right then?

Creative Writing Starters
Language Arts

I feel like running away when _____ .

I like to help out by _____ .

Sometimes people in my family tell me "not now" when

I _____.

I like to _____ on a "do-something" day.

Story Titles

Not Now

The Day I Ran Away

My New Job

Categories
Language Arts

Divide the class into six groups. Assign each group the name of one of the shops mentioned in the story:

> Carl's Garage
>
> Dimple's Delicatessen
>
> Bertha's Bakery
>
> Mr. Pfeffer's Fresh Produce
>
> Tom's Shoe Repair
>
> Byrd's Pet Shop

Encourage children to brainstorm and make a list of items that would be found in that shop. Add a time limit to spark quick thinking. Invite groups to share their lists with the class. Give each child a 3" x 5" card to draw a picture of one item from the list and write the item's name at the bottom of the card. Collect the cards and put them all in a lunch bag. Write the six shop names in columns on the chalkboard. Invite one student at a time to come to the front of the room, choose a card from the bag, and place it under the correct heading on the chalkboard.

Bernie's Neighborhood Runaway
Language Arts

Give each child a copy of the "Bernie's Neighborhood Runaway" reproducible on page 48 and a copy of the words and pictures on page 49. Have children cut the words and pictures apart on the dotted lines and glue them in the correct places on the chart to show how Bernie helped his friends and what his friends gave him. After children have finished, read the story again so that they can check their answers.

Something-to-Do Calculations
Math

Give each child a copy of the "Something-to-Do Calculations" reproducible on page 50. Have children compute the math problems. Encourage children to make up some math problems of their own based on facts from the story.

Definite Directions
Social Studies

Arrange student desks in traditional rows with aisles in between each desk. Assign different desks to be Bernie's house, Carl's Garage, Dimple's Delicatessen, Bertha's Bakery, Mr. Pfeffer's Fresh Produce, Tom's Shoe Repair, and Byrd's Pet Shop. Establish which directions will be north, south, east, and west, and post signs on the walls. The aisles between desks can be the streets of Bernie's neighborhood, and each desk can stand for one city block. Invite one student to stand in the middle of the room. Have another student direct him or her to one of the locations, such as Bertha's Bakery, using direction words: "Go three blocks north. Face west. Walk three blocks. Go five blocks north." Give each student a chance to give or follow directions.

Bernie's Neighborhood Runaway

Can you remember what Bernie did for each friend and what each friend gave him? Glue the correct words or picture in each box.

PLACE	HOW BERNIE HELPED	WHAT BERNIE GOT
Carl's Garage		
Dimple's Delicatessen		
Bertha's Bakery		
Pfeffer's Fresh Produce		
Tom's Shoe Repair		
Byrd's Pet Shop		

The Do-Something Day

Cut the words and pictures apart on the dotted lines. Glue them in the correct places on "Bernie's Neighborhood Runaway" chart to show how Bernie helped his friends and what Bernie's friends gave him.

handed Mr. Dimple salamis	
gave horse water	
fed fish and birds	
told Carl when the headlights went off and on	
delivered shoes to Bertha	
stamped the date on paper bags and stacked them	

The Do-Something Day

Something-to-Do Calculations

Read each problem carefully and answer the questions.

1. Mr. Dimple had 16 salamis hanging when Bernie came to help. Bernie handed him 5 more to hang.
   How many salamis were hanging when the job was done? _____

2. Bertha baked 7 loaves of rye bread, 6 loaves of french bread, and 2 loaves of spoon bread.
   How many loaves did she bake in all?_____

3. Mr. Pfeffer's wagon had grapes, bananas, carrots, potatoes, squash, lettuce, and melons on it. The vegetables sold for 20¢ per pound. The fruits sold for 25¢ per pound.
   How many pounds of fruit could you buy for 2 dollars?_____
   How much would 5 pounds of vegetables cost?_____

4. Mrs. Byrd has 5 cats, 4 dogs, 1 monkey, and 15 birds.
   How many pets does she have in all? _____

5. Bernie's father used the map to plan their trip. It was 17 miles one way to the fair.
   How many miles did Bernie and his family travel round trip? _____

The Do-Something Day

Very Last First Time

Written by Jan Andrews and illustrated by Ian Wallace
New York: Atheneum, 1986

Synopsis

In winter, the Inuit people in northern Canada collect mussels from the bottom of the seabed. For the very first time, Eva is going under the sea ice to collect mussels alone. Eva displays the common emotions of excitement, nervousness, fear, and a sense of accomplishment associated with a first-time experience.

Introduction

Ask the children if they remember the very first time they went to school or the first time they did something else. Ask them how the first-time experience made them feel. After you have done something once, you can never again say it is your very first time to do it. That first time is the "very last first time." Encourage the children to listen closely as the story is read aloud to find out what Eva does for the "very last first time."

Critical-Thinking and Discussion Questions

1. For the first time in her life, Eva Padlyat was going to walk on the bottom of the sea, and she was very excited. Can you remember a time when you did something for the first time all by yourself? What was it? How did you feel?
2. Eva decided to explore a rock pool after she finished her work. What are some things Eva found there? Where would you like to explore? What would you find there?
3. When Eva's candle dropped and sputtered out, she realized that she had gone too far. She was alone in the darkness. What did Eva do first when she realized she had a problem? Would you have done the same thing? What do you usually do first when you have a problem?
4. After finding her way back to the ice hole, Eva danced for joy. She skipped and leapt because she was so happy. In what ways do you show your happiness? What are some things you have done that made you happy?
5. Eva lived in northern Canada. (Point out Canada on a map.) How is the place Eva lived different from where you live? How is it the same?
6. After collecting the mussels by herself, Eva said that it was her "very last first time." Do you think Eva will be as nervous or excited to collect mussels alone the next time? Why or why not?

Creative Writing Starters

Language Arts

The first time I _____ I felt _____ .
I would like to explore _____ .
I felt very happy when _____ .
I remember the "very last first time" I _____ .

Story Titles
The First Time
All By Myself
I Can't Believe I Did It!

Word Whiz

Language Arts

Review the vocabulary words from the story that are listed on the "Word Whiz" reproducible on page 54. Be sure children are familiar with each word's meaning. Encourage students to use the words in original sentences. Give each child a copy of the "Word Whiz" reproducible. The children identify which words are nouns (people, places, or things) and which are verbs (action words) and write them in ABC order in the correct column.

Scrimshaw in Plastic

Art

Scrimshaw is an old form of folk art done by sailors to help pass the time on long voyages. Small carvings and engravings were scratched into the surface of whalebone, ivory, or wood. Then the engraved lines were colored with ink. Give each child a cottage cheese carton lid with the edge cut off, a nail, a paper towel, and crayons. Using the nail, children can scratch designs on the blank side of the lid and then color over the surface with crayon. Have the children rub off the excess crayon with a dry paper towel. Make the scrimshaw art pieces into necklaces by punching a hole in each lid and threading a piece of yarn through the hole.

Ice Cap

Science

In very cold climates, such as northern Canada, the top of the sea freezes solid. When the tide goes out, an ice cap remains over the seabed. To simulate this natural phenomenon for students, fill a plastic bowl with water. Put it in the freezer until the top $1/4''$ to $1/2''$ freezes. Remove the bowl from the freezer and poke a small hole in the ice. Drain out the water underneath.

False Facts

Science

Divide the class into five groups. Assign each group one of Eva's seabed discoveries:

mussels anemones crab
shrimps seaweed

Give each group the same number of 3" x 5" cards as there are group members. Provide books or encyclopedias that students can use to gather information about their assigned topic. The groups each research and write a one-sentence fact about their topic on all but one of their 3" x 5" cards. On the last 3" x 5" card, have students make up and write a false fact about their topic. When research is completed, choose one group to stand while each group member reads one fact. Invite the other class members to vote on the fact they think is the false one. It may be helpful to the voters to have the facts read more than once. After the class has voted, the group can reveal the false fact. Continue until all groups have had a turn.

Word Whiz

Circle each word below that is a verb. Underline each word that is a noun. Write the verbs in ABC order in the verb column. Write the nouns in ABC order in the noun column.

swallow	reach	stones	pull
wander	breathe	village	parka
shadow	hum	tundra	
explore	candle	seabed	

VERBS   NOUNS

About Me © 1991 Fearon Teacher Aids

Alexander, Who Used to Be Rich Last Sunday

Written by Judith Viorst and illustrated by Ray Cruz
New York: Atheneum, 1978

Synopsis

After Alexander receives a dollar from Grandma Betty and Grandpa Louie, he feels rich. Alexander is positively going to save his money. But after the irresistible temptations of bubble gum, chocolate candy, and a garage sale, Alexander and his money are soon parted.

Introduction

Show children a dollar bill and ask them what they would do with it if they received it as a gift. Ask children if they would rather save it or spend it. Alexander receives some money as a gift. Encourage children to listen closely as the story is read aloud to find out what Alexander chooses to do with his money.

Critical-Thinking and Discussion Questions

1. Alexander thought it was unfair that his brothers had more money than he did. Do you agree or disagree? Why do you think the brothers had more money? Have you ever felt that it was unfair that your brother, sister, or friend had more of something than you did?
2. Alexander tried very hard to save his money, but the temptation to spend was irresistible. If you had one dollar in your pocket, what would be an irresistible spending temptation to you?
3. Nicholas and Anthony teased Alexander. Alexander's angry reactions got him into trouble. How do you think Alexander should have handled the boys' teasing? What would you have done in Alexander's place?
4. Alexander tried to make money by returning nonreturnable bottles and pulling out teeth that weren't loose, neither of which worked. What are some good ways to make money?
5. Compare the way Alexander felt about his dollar in the beginning of the story with the way he felt at the end of the story. Compare yourself to Alexander. In what ways are you like him? In what ways are you different?

Creative Writing Starters

Language Arts

Saving money is hard because _____ .
If I had all the money I wanted, I would _____ .
I think _____ is a good way to earn money.
I like to buy _____ .

Story Titles

The Case of the Disappearing Dollar
How to Be Very Rich
The Bet I Never Win

What a Deal!

Language Arts

Remind children of Cathy's garage sale in the story. She used the sale as a way to get rid of the things she no longer wanted and to make some money. Show children some classified ads from the newspaper. Talk about the important information each ad contains. Have each child create an ad to advertise the sale of something they no longer want.

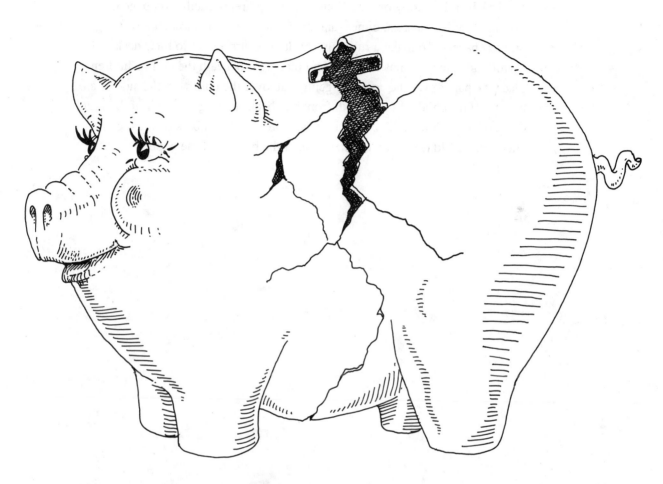

Absolutely, Positively
Language Arts

Several times Alexander said, "I absolutely positively was saving the rest of my money. But then . . . " He had good intentions, but spending the money was just too much fun. Encourage each child to use the sentence pattern and share an idea aloud with the class of an irresistible spending temptation. "I absolutely positively was saving the rest of my money. But then I saw this pack of baseball cards as I was walking out of the store."

Spending Countdown
Math

Give each child a copy of the "Spending Countdown" reproducible on page 59. Read through the book again and have children record each time Alexander spends his money and what he buys. Have children subtract the amount of purchase from the cash on hand before continuing on. If the math calculations are correct, the children should figure at the end of the story that Alexander has nothing left to spend but bus tokens!

Coin Collecting

Art

Give each child a copy of the "Coin Collecting" reproducible on page 60.
Provide pennies, nickels, dimes, and quarters for students to make rubbings
on their papers. To make a rubbing, children secure a coin to their desk top
by rolling a piece of masking tape and placing it beneath the coin. Children
place the paper over the coin and gently rub over the coin with the side of a
crayon. Have children make both front and back rubbings of each of the four
coins. Help children notice the pictures, words, and numbers on each coin.
Have each child design an original coin at the bottom of the paper.

Name _____

Spending Countdown

Alexander began with one dollar and soon had no money left. As you listen to the story again, record each time Alexander spends some money and the reason why. Subtract to find out how much money Alexander has left each time.

	AMOUNT SPENT	REASON	CASH LEFT
			$1.00
10	15¢	bubble gum	85¢
9			
8			
7			
6			
5			
4			
3			
2			
1			

Name _____

Coin Collecting

Use a crayon to make a rubbing of the front and back of each coin listed below. Design your own coin at the bottom of the page.

PENNY	**NICKEL**
DIME	**QUARTER**

My own coin: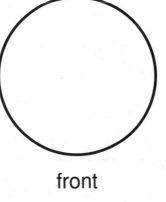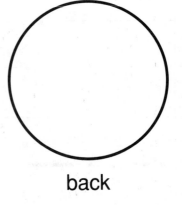

front   back

Alexander, Who Used to Be Rich Last Sunday

Nothing to Do

Written by Russell Hoban and illustrated by Lillian Hoban
New York: Harper & Row, 1964

Synopsis

Walter cannot think of anything to do, so Walter's father gives him a something-to-do stone. Walter has several adventures through the day and learns the valuable skill of thinking for himself.

Introduction

Ask children if they have ever been bored and had nothing to do. Ask children if they ever ask their moms or dads for ideas on what to do. Walter Possum has nothing at all to do. Invite children to listen closely as the story is read aloud to find out if he conquers his boredom problem.

Critical-Thinking and Discussion Questions

1. When was the last time you felt like Walter with nothing to do? What did you do about it? Did you have any of the same ideas that Walter had? What were some ideas you had that were similar to Walter's? In what ways did you act differently than Walter?
2. If Walter had come to you and said he had nothing to do, what would you have suggested to him?
3. Walter said that raking leaves wasn't really something to do. What do you think he meant by that?
4. Do you think the something-to-do stone worked for Walter? Why do you think that? Why was Walter still able to think of ideas to do after he lost the stone? What do you think the stone did for him? Do you think a something-to-do stone would work for you the next time you have nothing to do?
5. How did Charlotte feel about her brother at the beginning of the story? How did she feel about Walter at the end? Why did her attitude change toward Walter? In what ways are you like Charlotte?
6. Walter learned to think for himself and solve his own problems. He came up with some good ideas, including how to keep his sister busy. Have you ever come up with a really good idea? What was it?

Creative Writing Starters
Language Arts

When I have nothing to do, I _____ .
My mom or dad usually tell me to _____ when I have nothing to do.
When I think real hard, I _____ .
My best friend and I like to _____ .

Story Titles
My Bright Idea
The Magic Stone
Too Much to Do!

Pen Pal Letter
Language Arts

Give each child a copy of the "Pen Pal Letter" reproducible on page 64.
Have each child write a letter to a real or imaginary friend as if they were
Walter or Charlotte and tell about the something-to-do stone or the play-
right-here stick.

Brainstorm Brilliance
Language Arts

Children often complain that they have nothing to do when they have
finished their assigned work in the classroom or when they are on the
playground at recess. Use this opportunity to remind students of appropriate
activity choices, and encourage them to think of some new ideas. List all
suggestions on the chalkboard. After recess or a free period, ask children to
talk about the activity they chose.

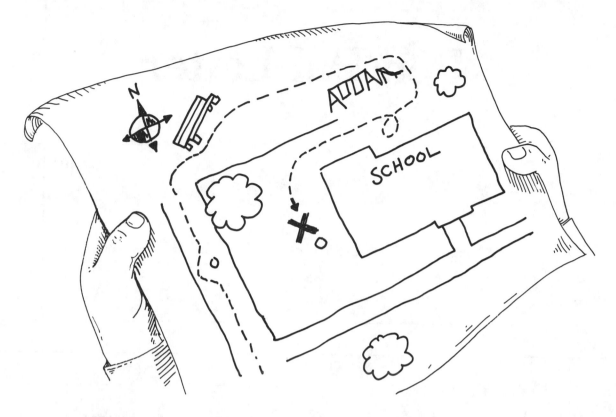

Treasure Maps
Art

Ask students to recall what happened when Kenneth and Walter played treasure in the story. Divide the class into small groups. Have each group decide on a "treasure" and a place to hide it on the school grounds. Invite each group to make a map that leads to their hidden treasure. Encourage students to be as accurate and clear as possible so that the treasures are not lost forever! Each group can hide their treasure. Have groups exchange maps and the treasure hunts can begin. It might be wise to set a time limit. If a group is unsuccessful at finding a treasure, encourage the group that made the map to give additional clues.

Look-Right-Here Circle
Science

Charlotte noticed some things by her play-right-here stick that she might never have seen if she had not taken the time to look closely. Give each child a 36" piece of yarn or string. Have students tie the two ends of their string together to make a look-right-here circle. Invite students to take their string circle, a piece of paper, and a pencil outside. Ask students to lay their string down on the ground and then carefully study the area inside the string for 5 minutes. Have students record their observations on the piece of paper. When the 5 minutes are up, come back into the classroom and discuss some of the finds. Find out how many observations each child made and ask each child to tell about the one observation he or she thought was most interesting. Ask students to compare their experiences to Charlotte's.

Pen Pal Letter

_____
Date

Dear _____ ,

_____

_____

_____

_____

_____

_____

_____

_____

_____

_____

_____

_____

                        _____ ,

                        _____

Nothing to Do

Because I Am Human

Written by Leo Buscaglia with photography by Bruce Ferguson
New York: Holt, Rinehart and Winston, 1972

Synopsis

The simple words and choice photographs represent a celebration of basic human pleasures and accomplishments, such as a mouthful of bubble gum, listening to a stream, and falling down without crying.

Introduction

Whistle and then snap your fingers. Explain that you can do those things because you are human. Ask children what they think it means to be human. Ask children what they can do because they are human. Encourage children to listen carefully as the words are read aloud and to enjoy the pictures in the book, *Because I Am Human.*

Critical-Thinking and Discussion Questions

1. Can you do all the things mentioned in the book? What are the things you can't do or have never tried? What are some things you can do that are not mentioned in the book?
2. (Show children the "I Can Climb A Tree . . . " page.) How do you think the boy in the picture is feeling? Why? How do you think the girl in the picture is feeling? Why? What are some things the children might be able to see while up in the tree that they could not see from the ground?
3. (Show children the "I Can Make A Wish . . . " page.) What do you think the boy is wishing for? If you could have one wish, what would it be?
4. (Show children the "I Can Do Things For Myself . . . " page.) What are some things that you can now do all by yourself that you used to ask for help to do?
5. Why do you think the author decided to write a book about things people can do? Are the things the author wrote about hard to do? (Share the information in the front of the book with the children about how the author got the idea to write the book.)

Creative Writing Starters

Language Arts

I can _____ .
I feel happy when _____ .
I can _____ all by myself.
When I fall down I usually _____ .
I believe in _____ .

Story Titles
High in the Tree
Look at Me!
The Wish

I Can . . .

Language Arts and Art

Give each child a 9" x 12" sheet of white construction paper. Have the children fold the papers in half and then unfold them. On the right side of the paper, children can draw a picture of themselves doing something they can do. On the left side of the paper, children can write an "I Can . . . " sentence about the picture or dictate the sentence for you to write for them. Encourage each child to share his or her picture and sentence with the class.

I Can Do That!

Language Arts

Divide children into groups of four. Give each group a copy of the "I Can Do That!" reproducible on page 68 and 69, a game spinner, and four game markers. All players begin with their markers on "Start." The first player spins and moves his or her marker the number of spaces indicated. Each player does the activity described on the space where the marker lands. Players take turns until each player reaches the finish line.

My Five Senses

Science

As humans, we experience things around us through our five senses. We can see, smell, feel, hear, and touch. Write the five senses on the chalkboard and then read through the book again with the children. Invite children to relate each page to one or more of their senses. For example, the girl on the first page is using her sense of smell to enjoy a flower. Give each child a copy of the "Five Senses Cube" reproducible on page 70. Have children color the pictures in each square. Children can cut the cube out on the outer lines, crease each solid line, and glue the tabs in place to make a three-dimensional cube. Divide children into groups of four or five. In turn, each child can throw his or her cube in the air and watch it land. If the cube lands with the taste side up, for example, the child can name something he or she likes to taste. If the cube lands with the "My Five Senses" side up, the child can try to name all five senses. Play continues until children have had the opportunity to share many of their favorite things.

I Car

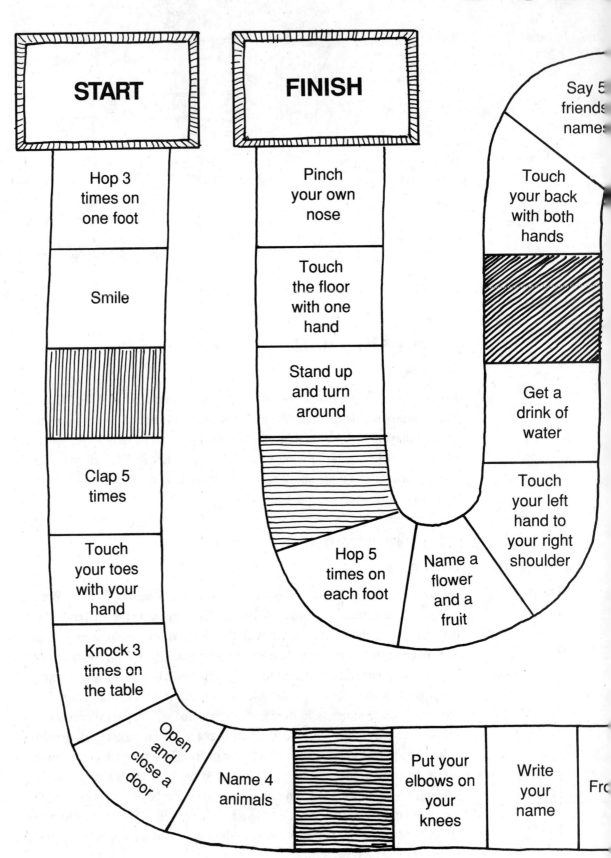

START

FINISH

Hop 3 times on one foot

Smile

Clap 5 times

Touch your toes with your hand

Knock 3 times on the table

Open and close a door

Name 4 animals

Pinch your own nose

Touch the floor with one hand

Stand up and turn around

Hop 5 times on each foot

Name a flower and a fruit

Put your elbows on your knees

Write your name

Fro

Say 5 friends names

Touch your back with both hands

Get a drink of water

Touch your left hand to your right shoulder

Because I Am Human

Do That!

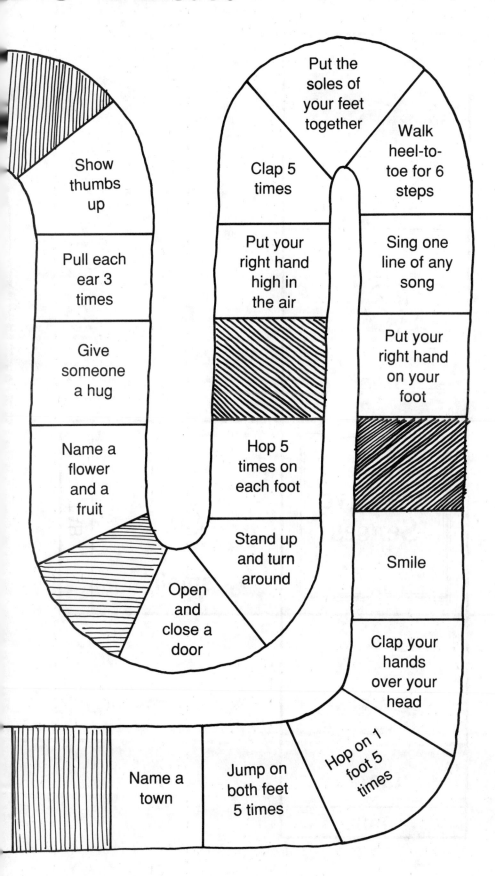

- Put the soles of your feet together
- Walk heel-to-toe for 6 steps
- Show thumbs up
- Clap 5 times
- Sing one line of any song
- Pull each ear 3 times
- Put your right hand high in the air
- Put your right hand on your foot
- Give someone a hug
- Hop 5 times on each foot
- Name a flower and a fruit
- Stand up and turn around
- Smile
- Open and close a door
- Clap your hands over your head
- Name a town
- Jump on both feet 5 times
- Hop on 1 foot 5 times

About Me © 1991 Fearon Teacher Aids

Five Senses Cube

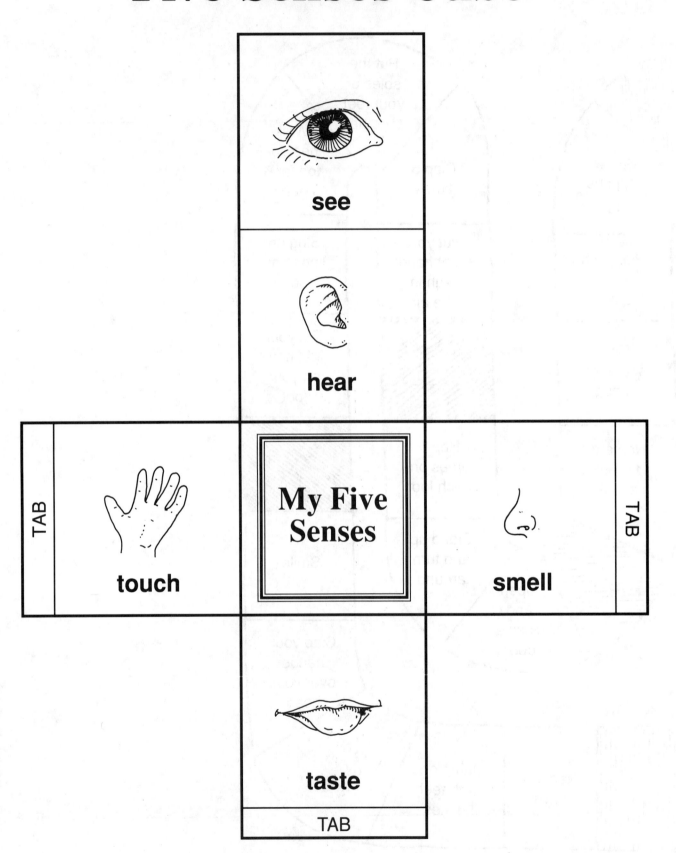

see

hear

TAB

touch

My Five
Senses

smell

TAB

taste

TAB

About Me © 1991 Fearon Teacher Aids

Because I Am Human

Spectacles

Written and illustrated by Ellen Raskin
New York: Macmillan Publishing, 1968

Synopsis

Iris sees some unusual things that other people don't, such as a fire-breathing dragon, a fat kangaroo, and an Indian making funny faces. That is, other people don't see things *in the same way* Iris does. Finally, Iris's mom takes her to the eye doctor and after some resistance to wearing glasses, Iris realizes that she enjoys seeing things the way they are supposed to look.

Introduction

Explain that *spectacles* is another word for *glasses*. Have children look closely at the two pictures on the front cover of the book and ask them how the two pictures are alike. Explain that both pictures are of the same things. The top picture is how Iris sees things and the bottom picture is the way everyone else sees things. Encourage children to look closely at each picture in the book as the story is read aloud to discover why Iris saw the unusual things she did. You might want to reread the story so that children can appreciate the pictures and look more closely at the details.

Critical-Thinking and Discussion Questions

1. Do you think Iris realized that she had problems seeing correctly when she saw things like giant caterpillars and fire-breathing dragons? What did she do about it? What would you do if you noticed something was not right with your eyes or another part of your body?
2. Iris said "No" to wearing glasses. Why do you think she felt that way? How would you feel if you were told that you had to wear glasses? What would you do?
3. No one seemed to notice that Iris looked different with her glasses except Chester. Have you ever been worried that your friends would tease you because you looked different? What would you do if someone teased you?
4. How do you think wearing glasses will change Iris's life?
5. How do you think Iris will treat other people she sees who wear glasses? How do you treat people who look differently than you?

Creative Writing Starters

Language Arts

I take good care of my eyes by _____ .

One day I thought a _____ looked like a _____.

The best thing about wearing glasses would be _____.

I thought everybody would notice I looked different when _____.

I think doctors are _____ because _____ .

Story Titles

The Day Iris Lost Her Glasses

Chester Visits the Optician

The Amazing Spectacles

Designer Frames

Art

Give each child a copy of the "Designer Frames" reproducible on page 74. Encourage children to design an original pair of spectacles. After all the pieces are cut out, children can tape the ear pieces to the sides of the frames to make the glasses wearable.

The "Eyes" Have It
Health

Encourage children to think of ways to take good care of their eyes. Make a list on the chalkboard. Your list may include the following:

Eat plenty of foods rich in vitamin A, such as carrots and apricots.

Read in a well-lit area.

Rest your eyes when you are reading or working on the computer for a long period of time.

Give each child a 12" x 18" sheet of white construction paper to design a poster illustrating an important message about eye care. Display the posters around the classroom or school to remind students about proper eye care.

Your Amazing Eyes
Science

Discuss with students how our eyes often "play tricks" on us. Read Ed Emberley's *The Wizard of Op* to the children to introduce them to the art of optical illusion. Discuss some of the special characteristics of our eyes, such as persistence of vision. Our eyes are able to hold an image in memory even after we are no longer looking at the image. To demonstrate this concept, give each student two 3" x 5" cards. Have students draw part of a picture on one card and the other part on the other card. For example, a student could draw a bird cage in the center of one card and a bird in the center of another. Or, a student could draw a fishbowl on one card and a fish on another. After drawing, students secure both cards back-to-back with the pictures facing out and glue or tape the eraser end of a pencil between the cards. Students can use the pencil as a handle by holding it between their palms and twisting briskly. The two images on the twirling cards will blend together to form a single picture. (Caution students that both images must be in the center of the cards or they will not blend together in the right positions.)

Designer Frames

Design your own pair of unique spectacles.

About Me © 1991 Fearon Teacher Aids

Ira Sleeps Over

Written by Bernard Waber
Boston: Houghton Mifflin, 1972

Synopsis

Ira's first sleep-over is at Reggie's house, but Ira can't decide if he should take his teddy bear. Will Reggie laugh if he does? Ira's sister says "yes" and his parents say "no." In the end, Ira learns that he and his friend have many things in common, including teddy bears.

Introduction

Show students an overnight bag in which you have prepacked a few items, such as a toothbrush and pajamas. Ask students to speculate about what you might have packed in the bag. Invite students to listen closely as the story is read aloud to find out what Ira takes with him on his first sleep-over.

Critical-Thinking and Discussion Questions

1. Ira was worried about taking his teddy bear to Reggie's house because Ira thought Reggie would laugh at him. Have you ever been worried about doing something because you might be laughed at? What was it? Did you do it anyway? If so, were you laughed at?
2. Reggie and Ira planned to have a pillow fight, play checkers, fool around with a magnifying glass, and tell ghost stories. What sorts of things would you plan to do if your friend could sleep over at your house?
3. Ira decided **not** to take his teddy bear to Reggie's house. Would you have made the same decision? Why or why not? Do you think Reggie would have laughed at Ira if he had brought the teddy bear?
4. At the end of the story, Ira changed his mind and went back to his house to get his teddy bear. What made Ira change his mind? Do you think Reggie was worried about letting Ira see that he slept with a teddy bear? Why or why not?
5. Ira's sister advised Ira **not** to take his teddy bear to Reggie's house. Ira's parents advised Ira **to** take the teddy bear and said that Reggie would not laugh. Whose advice did Ira follow? Who gave the best advice? Whose advice do you usually listen to?
6. What do you think happened the next morning when Reggie and Ira woke up?

Creative Writing Starters

Language Arts

When I sleep over at my friend's house I will bring _____ .
Teddy bears are fun because _____ .
Sometimes I am afraid of _____ .
I always do what _____ says because _____ .

Story Titles
My First Sleep-Over
The Best Advice
Teddy Bear Trouble
The Day I Followed My Sister's Advice

Silly Bear Names

Language Arts

Ask children if they can remember the names of Reggie's and Ira's teddy bears. Ask children if they have teddy bears and what the bears' names are. Give each child a copy of the "Silly Bear Names" reproducible on page 78. Have children think of a silly bear name that begins with each letter in the word *teddy bear*. Each child can circle his or her favorite name on the page and then draw a picture of that teddy bear.

Teddy Bear Booklets
Language Arts

Reproduce the teddy bear on page 79 on brown construction paper. Give each student one copy of the teddy bear, another sheet of brown construction paper, and a sheet of lined writing paper. Have the children stack the three sheets of paper with the writing paper in the middle and the teddy bear outline on top. Punch two holes in the top of the teddy bear's head and tie a red ribbon through the holes to make a booklet. Have students cut around the bear outline through all three sheets of paper to make the booklet bear shaped. Inside the booklet, children write five reasons why they do or do not own a teddy bear.

Bear Collage
Art

Give each child a copy of the bear outline reproducible on page 79. Provide children with collage materials, such as brown beans, wood shavings, macaroni, or brown rice. Have children spread glue over a small portion of the bear at a time and cover the glue with a textured collage material of their choice. Children can use construction paper to add facial features or clothing to the bear. Plastic rolling eyes add to the finished look.

Sleep-Over Schedule
Math

Give each child a copy of the "Sleep-Over Schedule" reproducible on page 80. Children can read about the activities the boys did the evening of the sleep-over and how long each activity lasted, or you can read the information aloud. Have children draw the hands on each clock to show what time it was when each activity ended and then write the times on the lines to the left of the clocks.

Name _____

Silly Bear Names

Think of a silly bear name that begins with each letter in the words **teddy bear.** Circle your favorite name and draw a picture of a teddy bear with that name.

T _____   B _____

E _____   E _____

D _____   A _____

D _____   R _____

Y _____

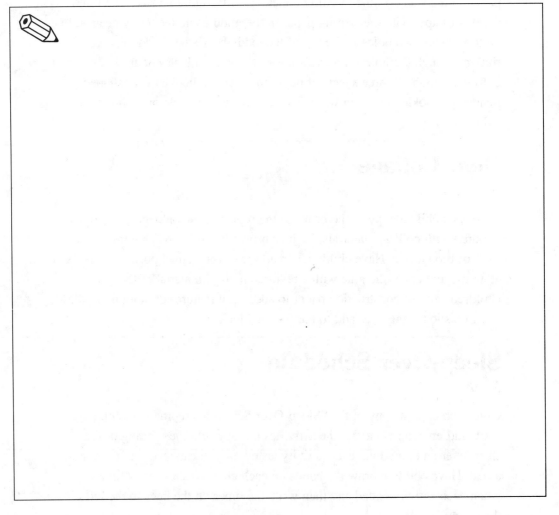

About Me © 1991 Fearon Teacher Aids

Ira Sleeps Over

Ira Sleeps Over

Sleep-Over Schedule

Draw the hands on the clock to show the time Ira and Reggie finished each activity. Write the time beside each clock.

1 Ira went to Reggie's house at 6:00.

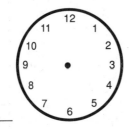

_____

2 The boys looked at Reggie's junk collection for 1 hour. What time was it then?

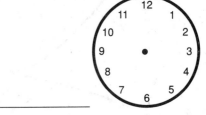

_____

3 They had a wrestling match that lasted ½ hour. What time was it then?

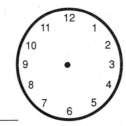

_____

4 Their pillow fight lasted 1 hour. What time was it when the pillow fight ended?

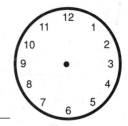

_____

5 Reggie's father told the boys to go to bed ½ hour after the pillow fight ended. What time was it then?

_____

6 One hour after the boys went to bed, Ira went home to get his teddy bear. What time was it then?

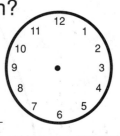

_____

On the back of your paper, draw a big clock to show what time you would go to bed if you had a sleep-over.

About Me © 1991 Fearon Teacher Aids

Ira Sleeps Over

Harry and the Terrible Whatzit

Written by Dick Gackenbach
New York: Seabury Press, 1977

Synopsis

Harry is sure his mother has been captured by a monster in the basement.
He overcomes his fear and goes down in the basement to rescue her. When
Harry faces his fear (the Whatzit), he realizes it isn't as big as he thought.

Introduction

Ask children to recall times they have been afraid and what kinds of things
frighten them. It might make them feel better to know that they are not
alone. Harry, the boy in the story, is afraid, too. Encourage children to listen
closely as the story is read aloud to find out what Harry does about his fear.

Critical-Thinking and Discussion Questions

1. Why did Harry think there must be something terrible down in the cellar?
   Have you ever been afraid to go someplace because of what you thought
   might be there? Did you go anyway? What did you see?
2. After Harry had waited for a while by the cellar door and his mother did
   not return, he decided to go down and find her. What does that tell you
   about Harry? Would you have acted in the same way? Why or why not?
3. Why did the Whatzit begin to shrink? Things that frighten us seem very
   big. But when we face them they often seem less frightening than we
   imagined them to be. Is there something that frightens you? What is it?
   What can you do to shrink it down to size?
4. Harry didn't think that his mother believed him when he told her about
   the Whatzit. Would you have believed Harry? Do you ever feel that
   people don't always believe what you say? Do you believe everything
   other people tell you?
5. At the end of the story, Harry heard an awful yell coming from the house
   next door. What do you think Sheldon will do about the Whatzit? What
   would you do?

Creative Writing Starters
Language Arts

I am afraid of _____ .
When I am afraid, I usually _____ .
No one believed me when I said that _____ .

Story Titles
Bravery at Its Best
The Dark, Damp Cellar
Would **You** Believe It?
The Horrible Whozit

Monsters I've Met
Language Arts

Talk with children about how the Whatzit was really Harry's fear of the unknown in the dark basement. Encourage children to share some of their fears (fear of the dark, being left alone, or visiting the dentist or doctor). Refer to these fears as the monsters the children have met. Give each child a copy of the "Monsters I've Met" reproducible on page 84. Invite children to write down three of their fears and imagine a monster that could represent one of their fears. Then have each child draw a picture of the monster in the box and give it a name. As an extension, give each child a sheet of writing paper to write a paragraph or short story about coming face-to-face with the monster and conquering it. Children can title their stories by using the same pattern as the book title—(child's name) and the Terrible (monster's name).

Ditto Art Monsters
Art

Give the students each a sheet of white drawing paper and have them use a pencil to draw a unique monster. Then give each student an inked backing from a used ditto. Have students place the inked sheet (ink side up) under the pencil drawing and carefully retrace it. After retracing, the students lift their drawings off the ink and set the ditto sheets aside. On the inked side of the monster pictures, students color their monsters, pressing firmly with bright crayons. The children can use white crayon for sections that they would like to remain uncolored. Caution students to color inside the inked lines and not on them. Provide a shallow tub of water for students to dip their monster pictures in after coloring. The purple ink will run and color all areas that are not covered by crayon. The stark contrast between the ink and the crayons will give the monsters an eery, creepy creature look. Lay the pictures on news-paper to dry.

Pickle Preparations
Science

Harry's mother went down to the cellar to get a jar of pickles. Ask children if they know how pickles are made. They might be surprised to know that pickles are made from cucumbers. Give the children each a slice of cucumber and a pickle to taste. Ask children to speculate what would have to be done to turn a cucumber into a pickle. Use the following recipe to make pickles with your class:

6 cucumbers	$1/4$ cup salt
2 small sprigs of dill	2 peppercorns
2 buds of garlic	2 cloves
1 gallon hot water	1 bay leaf
1 cup vinegar	

Wash and dry the cucumbers. Put one sprig of dill, one bud of garlic, one peppercorn, one clove, and the bay leaf into a big jar. Add the cucumbers and put the rest of the dill, garlic, peppercorn, and cloves on top.

Mix the water, salt, and vinegar to make a mixture called *brine*. Stir the mixture well. Add the brine to the cucumbers and put a plate on top to keep the cucumbers under the brine.

Let the cucumbers soak in the brine. In a few days, you will see foam on top of the brine. Remove the foam every day. The pickles will be ready in two to four weeks.

Monsters I've Met

Write down three of your fears. Draw a picture in the box of what one of your fears might look like if it were a monster. Write the monster's name on the line at the bottom of the box.

I am afraid of _____

_____

_____

_____

On another sheet of paper, write a short story about how you would conquer your monster.

About Me © 1991 Fearon Teacher Aids

Harry and the Terrible Whatzit

The Hating Book

Written by Charlotte Zolotow and illustrated by Ben Shecter
New York: Harper & Row, 1969

Synopsis

Two friends have a misunderstanding because one received some inaccurate information. Each thinks the other friend hates her. Through the wise advice of mother, the girls smooth their strained friendship by talking about the problem.

Introduction

Ask children if they have ever been mad at a friend and how they treated the friend when they were angry. Ask the children how they solved the problem. This story is about two friends who are mad at one another. Encourage children to listen closely as the story is read aloud to find out why the friends are mad and if they are able to solve the problem.

Critical-Thinking and Discussion Questions

1. The first little girl enjoyed doing many things with her friend, like walking home from school, playing with her dog, helping with chores, and playing basketball. She missed doing all of these things when she "hated" her friend. What would you miss most about your friends if you were mad at them?

2. The little girl's mother advised the little girl to ask her friend why she was ignoring her. Do you think that was good advice? What advice would you have given to the little girl?

3. The cause of the hurt feelings between the two girls was a misunderstanding. The little girl said that her friend looked neat, but the friend heard "secondhand" that she looked like a freak. Have you ever been told some "secondhand" information? Did you believe it? What would you do if what you heard hurt your feelings?

4. How do you think the misunderstanding between the two girls could have been avoided?

5. The girls solved their problem by talking about it. How do you solve the problems you have with your friends?

Creative Writing Starters
Language Arts

I thought my friend hated me when _____ .
My friend and I talk about _____ .
My friend and I like to _____ .
My friend makes me mad when he/she _____ .
When I am mad at my friend, I _____ .

Story Titles
My Best Friend
Things Are Not Always as They Seem
I'd Rather Be Your Friend

Mixed Messages
Language Arts

Have children sit in a circle. One child whispers a compliment about another child, such as "Jenny has pretty brown hair," in the ear of the person sitting to his or her right. The person who received the whispered message whispers it to the person to his or her right. Children continue to pass the whispered message until it has gone all the way around the circle. The last person to receive the message says it aloud. If the message is the same one that was started, congratulations! The children were good listeners and accurately conveyed what they heard. But more likely, the message will be altered. Relate this game to what happened in the story between the two friends.

Dear Annie
Language Arts

We often seek the advice of others when we have a problem to solve. The little girl's mother offered some advice that proved to be very wise. Have each student write a letter to "Annie" explaining a fictitious or very real problem they are having with a friend or family member. Students can sign the letters with an alias. Collect the letters and redistribute them randomly. Invite children to write a letter of reply offering some wise advice for solving the problem. Have several of the letters and replies read aloud.

Paper Plate Masks
Art

Give the children each a tongue depressor and two small paper plates. Have children draw a happy face on one plate and a sad or angry face on the other plate. Glue the tongue depressor to the back side of one plate to use as a handle. Staple the two plates together with the tongue depressor in the middle and the faces facing out. Children can work in groups to create scripts that express conversations friends often have and use the masks as props when they act out the scenarios.

Seasonal Signs

Science

Ask children if they noticed the type of weather depicted in the story and what season of the year it might have been. Make copies of the "Seasonal Signs" reproducible on page 88 for the children and ask them each to color and cut out the four cards. Discuss the names of the three months listed on each card and the weather conditions and holidays that occur in each season. Then ask the children some questions about the seasons and have them respond by holding up the appropriate card.

   When is the best time to build a snowman?
   When do many leaves fall from the trees?
   When would be a good time to pick a bouquet of flowers?
   What season is Thanksgiving in?
   In what season do you begin school each year?
   Which season would have plenty of nice hot days for swimming?

After asking questions, give each child a piece of white drawing paper. Have children glue the season cards on their papers in the order in which they occur during the year, beginning with the current season.

Seasonal Signs

Color and cut out the seasonal cards on the dotted lines.
Use the cards to answer some seasonal questions.

Fall

September, October, November

Summer

June, July, August

Spring

March, April, May

Winter

December, January, February

About Me © 1991 Fearon Teacher Aids

The Hating Book

William's Doll

Written by Charlotte Zolotow and illustrated by William Pène Du Bois
New York: Harper and Row, 1972

Synopsis

More than anything, William wanted a doll. His family bought him all sorts of other toys, hoping that his interest in a doll would wane. One day, someone finally understood William's request.

Introduction

Ask if any children have a favorite doll. Ask children what they enjoy doing with their dolls. Ask children if they think boys or girls more often play with dolls and why. Encourage children to listen carefully as the story is read aloud to find out why William wanted a doll.

Critical-Thinking and Discussion Questions

1. William wanted a doll, and no other toys he received satisfied that desire. Have you ever wanted something very badly? What was it? Did you get it? How did you feel?
2. Why did William's brother and the boy next door tease him for wanting a doll? Did William change his mind? Have you ever changed your mind because of someone else's opinion?
3. How do you think William's brother and friend will treat him now that he has a doll? Do you think they will still tease him? What would you do if someone teased you because of something you had or liked to do?
4. Why do you think William's grandmother understood his wishing for a doll? Do you have a grandparent, friend, or family member who seems to understand things about you that no one else does? Who is it? Why do you think they understand you so well?
5. William's grandmother agreed that he should have a doll so that he could practice being a father. Do you think that practice will help make William a good father? What are some ways you would try to be a good mother or father?

Creative Writing Starters
Language Arts

Once I wanted a _____ , but I got a _____ instead.
I wanted a _____ , but my parents said "No" because _____ .
Grandmothers and grandfathers are special because they _____ .
I think dolls are _____ .

Story Titles
The Doll That Came to Life
I Finally Got It!

A Note of Thanks
Language Arts

Give each child a copy of the letter form reproducible on page 93. Children can pretend to be William and write letters to the grandmother thanking her for the doll. Encourage children to think about how William must have felt. Help them express those thoughts to the grandmother.

Numerous Names
Language Arts

As a class, brainstorm and write a list on the chalkboard of possible names for William's doll. After children run out of ideas or the board is full, give them each a copy of the "Numerous Names" reproducible on page 94. The children can each choose ten of their favorite names from the board and write them down in the left-hand column of the paper. Then the children can recopy their ten favorite names in alphabetical order in the right-hand column.

Why Not?
Language Arts

Have students choose a partner to do this writing activity. Together the two partners choose a toy that they would want as badly as William wanted a doll. Have them write the name of the toy at the top of a sheet of lined writing paper and fold the paper in half lengthwise to create two columns. Have students label the left column "I want it because . . ." and label the right column "You can't have it because . . ." Encourage partners to brainstorm to- gether to think of as many reasons as possible why they want the toy and write the reasons in the left-hand column. Then have partners pretend to be in the parents' position and think of reasons they might be denied their request and write those reasons in the right-hand column. Partners can dramatize their thoughts for the class by having one student play the child and the other play the parent.

Make a Scene!

Art

Have each child cut out a picture of a boy and a doll from a magazine. (Christmas catalogs are a good source of pictures.) Children can glue the pictures on construction paper and draw the rest of the scene with crayons. Remind students how William felt when he finally got his doll and to think about all the things William wanted to do with his doll. Encourage children to draw pictures that portray these important parts of the story.

Dear Grandmother,

_____

_____

_____

_____

_____

_____

_____

_____

_____

_____

_____

Love,

William

Written by: _____

William's Doll

Numerous Names

Choose ten names for William's doll and write them
on the left side of your paper. Then recopy the names
in alphabetical order on the right side of your paper.

NAMES I LIKE	ALPHABETICAL ORDER
1. _____	1. _____
2. _____	2. _____
3. _____	3. _____
4. _____	4. _____
5. _____	5. _____
6. _____	6. _____
7. _____	7. _____
8. _____	8. _____
9. _____	9. _____
10. _____	10. _____

Circle the name you like the best.

About Me © 1991 Fearon Teacher Aids

William's Doll

Alexander and the Terrible, Horrible, No Good, Very Bad Day

Written by Judith Viorst and illustrated by Ray Cruz
New York: Atheneum, 1973

Synopsis

Alexander went to sleep with gum in his mouth, tripped on his skateboard, and dropped his sweater in the sink. He could tell that it was going to be one of those days when nothing seems to go right. But through the course of the amusingly horrible day, Alexander realizes that some days are just like that.

Introduction

Ask children if they have ever had a day when everything seemed to go wrong. Invite children to look carefully at the picture of Alexander on the cover of the book. Ask children what kind of day they think he has had and how they think he is feeling. Encourage children to listen closely as the story is read aloud to find out if they are right about Alexander's day.

Critical-Thinking and Discussion Questions

1. What are some of the things that happened to Alexander throughout the day, contributing to his terrible, horrible, no good, very bad day? Have any of these things ever happened to you? When?
2. Alexander hated lima beans. Is there a food that you hate? What do you do when this food is served to you? Do you think you will always hate this food, or will you someday change your mind?
3. Alexander seemed to think that his life would be better if he moved to Australia. Why do you think Alexander chose Australia? Do you think he could have troubles there? Why or why not? If you were having a horrible day, where would you choose to go?
4. Alexander's mother told him that some days are just like that. Do you agree? What advice would you have given to Alexander? Is there anything you can do to turn a horrible day into a good day?
5. The story ended with Alexander going to sleep. What do you think his day will be like tomorrow? Suppose tomorrow is just the opposite! What could happen to Alexander to make his day a "terrific, wonderful, not bad, very good day?"

Creative Writing Starters
Language Arts

If I were a parent of a child like Alexander, I would _____ .

I like being part of my family because _____ .

Sometimes it is hard for me to be happy around my family when _____ .

The worst day of my life was when _____ .

Story Titles

From Bad to Worse

Things Are Looking Up

Avoid, If Possible

Very Bad Day Comic Book
Language Arts

Give each child a copy of the "Very Bad Day" reproducible on page 99. Explain that the talk boxes provide space for two characters to talk to each other. Have children write dialogue between themselves and Alexander or themselves and a friend about a very bad day. Children can add illustrations when they have finished their scripts. Combine all the pages to make a "Very Bad Day" class comic book. Add a title page and a table of contents to help each author find his or her page in the book. (You might find it advantageous to write a script together as a class before children start to do their own.)

Meet a Friend

Language Arts

Have children recall Alexander's likes and dislikes mentioned in the story. Give each child a copy of the "Meet a Friend" reproducible on page 100. Read the form with the class to be sure all the questions are clear. Have children choose partners and interview each other, recording the friend's likes and dislikes. Have children read the information from their sheets aloud to the class to introduce their partners.

Shoe Toppers

Art

Remind children how Alexander thought that wearing plain old white sneakers was horrible. He wanted to buy blue ones with red stripes, but the shoe man said that they were sold out. Give each child two copies of the "Shoe Topper" reproducible on page 101 to decorate. Have children cut out the shoe toppers and cut slits on the solid lines at the toe end. Overlap the slit sections to the dotted lines and glue in place to round the toe end of the toppers. Have children cut out the strip and staple or tape end A to side A of the topper and then fit it around the back of the heel and staple or tape end B to side B of the topper.

The Great Getaway

Geography

Give each student a copy of the world map reproducible on page 102. Have students locate and write in the names of the seven continents. Point out Alexander's location for a great getaway (Australia). Children can circle the place that they consider to be a great getaway and then write a paragraph at the bottom of the page explaining why.

Very Bad Day

by _____

1 | **2**

3 | **4**

Alexander and the Terrible, Horrible, No Good, Very Bad Day

Name _____

Meet a Friend

My friend: _____

Interviewed by: _____

Where do you live? _____

Who lives at your house? _____

_____

Do you have any pets? What kind? _____

_____

What happens on TV that you dislike? _____

_____

What foods do you dislike? _____

_____

What is your favorite cereal? _____

What is your favorite dessert? _____

Alexander and the Terrible, Horrible, No Good, Very Bad Day

Shoe Topper

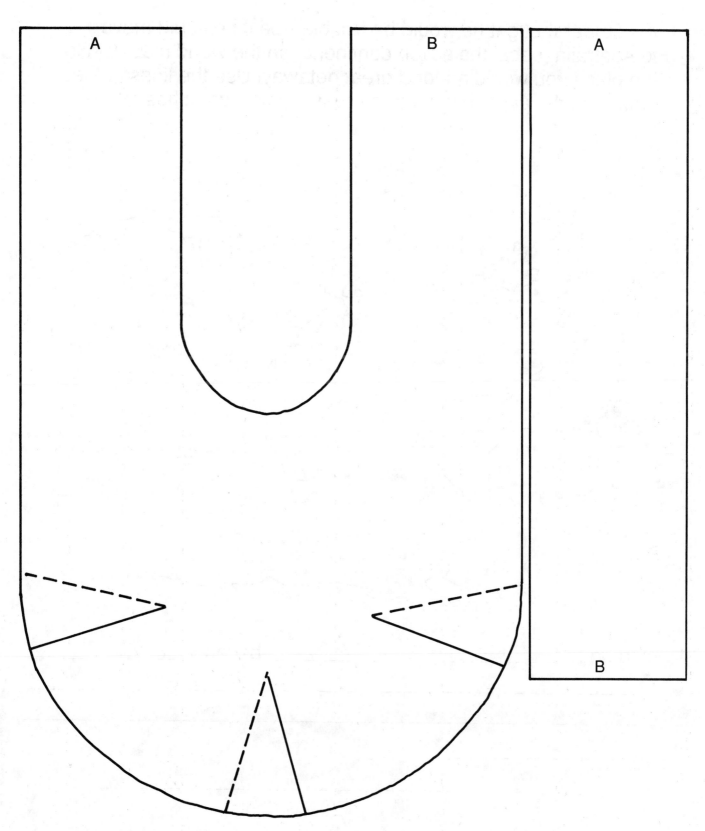

Alexander and the Terrible, Horrible, No Good, Very Bad Day

Name _____

The Great Getaway

Alexander thought he would be trouble-free if he could move to Australia. Label the seven continents on the world map. Circle the place you would go for a great getaway. Use the lines at the bottom of the page to write three reasons why you chose that place.

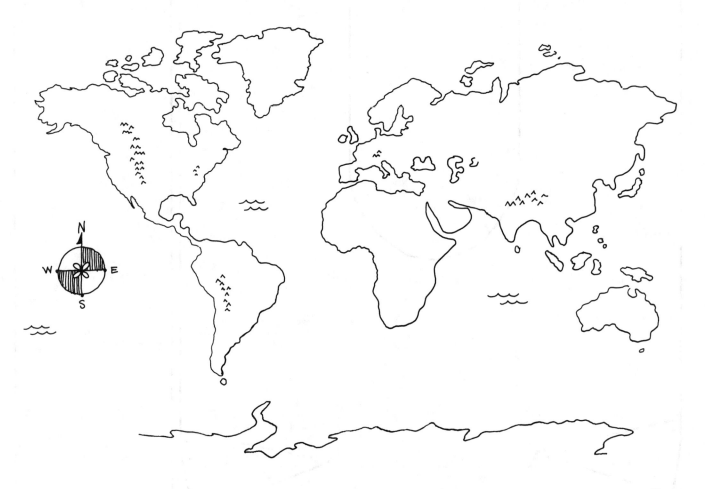

I would go to _____ because _____

_____

_____

_____

_____

Alexander and the Terrible, Horrible, No Good, Very Bad Day

About Me © 1991 Fearon Teacher Aids

Oliver Button Is a Sissy

Written and illustrated by Tomie de Paola
New York: Harcourt Brace Jovanovich, 1979

Synopsis

Oliver likes to do something that not many boys have tried—dance. Some of his fellow classmates tease him, but that doesn't stop Oliver. He continues to practice and enjoy his dancing and finally enters a talent show. Oliver doesn't win first prize, but his disappointment is short-lived because he gains the respect of his classmates.

Introduction

Ask children what they think a "sissy" is. Encourage children to listen carefully as the story is read aloud to find out why Oliver is called a "sissy."

Critical-Thinking and Discussion Questions

1. What are some things that Oliver liked to do? Which of those things do you also enjoy doing?
2. Oliver didn't like to play ball because he wasn't very good at it. He was always the last person picked for the team. Is there something you don't like to do because you don't think you're very good at it? What is it? Have you ever been chosen last for a team? If so, how did you feel?
3. Oliver's parents didn't think he was getting enough exercise, but Oliver reminded his mother that he liked to jump rope and dance. What do you like to do for exercise?
4. Why did the other boys think Oliver was a sissy? Do you think he was a sissy? Why or why not?
5. Oliver entered a talent contest as a dancer. If you could enter a talent contest, what would you like to do?
6. When Oliver heard that he did not win first prize in the contest, he tried not to cry. How do you feel and what do you do when you don't win a contest, game, or race? How important is winning to you? Oliver's friends thought he was a star even though he did not win first prize. Do you agree? Why?

Creative Writing Starters
Language Arts

When teams are being chosen, I usually _____ .
Kids who call other kids "sissy" are _____ .
I am good at _____ .
Name-calling is _____ .

Story Titles
My Night in the Spotlight
Practice, Practice, Practice
That First Dance Class

Class Talent Show
Language Arts

A class talent show can provide children with the opportunity to enhance their communication skills and participate in a group experience. Divide the class into groups of four or five students. Encourage each group to decide on a skit, song, or puppet play that they will present to the class. Be sure to remind children to include each group member in the performance. Children can design show programs and invite parents or other schoolmates to attend the performance.

Patterned Applause
Language Arts

The audience clapped and clapped for Oliver. Give your students some clapping exercises that will strengthen their ability to listen and follow a sequence. Ask students to listen closely while you clap a pattern. Then have students repeat it back. For example, clap three times quickly, two times slowly. Continue using a variety of rhythm and beats with other clapping patterns, according to your students' abilities. Ask individual volunteers to repeat patterns alone or make up and demonstrate clapping patterns for the class to repeat.

Spotlight Stars
Art

Give each child an 8 ½" x 11" sheet of black construction paper, a 6" paper plate, and a sheet of white drawing paper. Have the children use the plate as a pattern to trace a circle on the black construction paper. The children can cut out the 6" circle and glue the white drawing paper to the back of the black paper to create a spotlight effect. Invite children to draw themselves in the spotlight doing something they consider to be their talent. Children can use a piece of white chalk or a white crayon to write "(child's name) in the Spotlight" at the top of the page. Combine all pages in a class book entitled "Spotlight Stars."

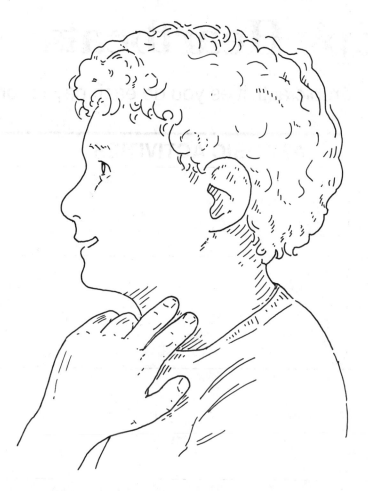

Happy Heartbeats

Science

Oliver's mother was worried that he was not getting enough exercise. However, Oliver reminded his mother that he liked to walk, jump rope, and dance. Explain to children that these activities and many others that cause them to breathe harder and faster are called aerobic exercise. The heart muscle is strengthened as it beats faster to supply the body with necessary oxygen during aerobic exercise. Show children how to take their resting pulse rates by placing two fingers over the carotid artery, located in the neck, just below the jawline, and counting the beats for an interval of ten seconds. (If some children cannot find their pulse, encourage them to feel the pulse in your neck and then help them locate their own pulse.) Have the children jog in place for three minutes and then check their pulse rates again. Talk about the difference in the resting pulse rate and the pulse rate after aerobic exercise. Make a list on the chalkboard of other activities the children name that cause their hearts to beat faster. Give each child a copy of the "Happy Heartbeats" reproducible on page 106. Invite children to keep a record of the aerobic activities they do for one week. After the week is up, discuss how students feel about the amount of exercise they are getting.

Name _____

Happy Heartbeats

Keep a record of the aerobic activities you do each day for one week.

DAY	AEROBIC ACTIVITIES
1	
2	
3	
4	
5	
6	
7	

About Me © 1991 Fearon Teacher Aids

Oliver Button Is a Sissy